The Triceratops and the Crocodiles

Story by Hugh Price   Illustrations by Ben Spiby

A long, long time ago, some enormous dinosaurs lived in a forest.

They were called triceratops, and each one had three big horns on its head.

Triceratops liked to eat lots of green leaves.

But one year there was no rain at all.
The forest was very dry.
The leaves on the trees turned brown.

The triceratops had to go away from the forest to find food. They went to look for a place where there were lots of green leaves.

The triceratops walked along together.
Their babies were in the middle of the herd.

Soon they all had to cross a wide river.

There were hungry crocodiles waiting in the water.

Some of the biggest triceratops moved down to the river very fast. They made the ground shake as they ran.

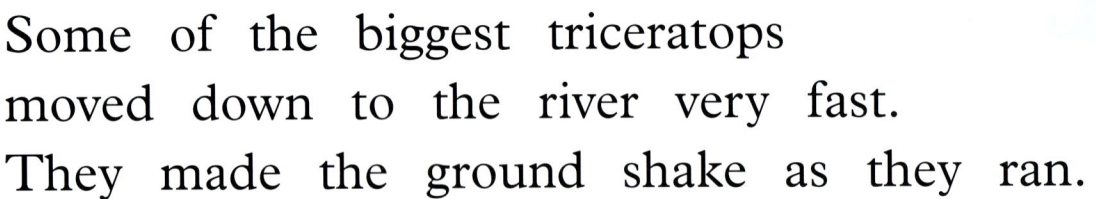

Their heavy legs made enormous splashes as they went into the water.

The crocodiles slid out of the way in a hurry. These triceratops were too big to catch.

The biggest triceratops
could keep their heads above the water.
They didn't need to swim.
They could **walk** across the river.

But the small ones had to swim.

One baby triceratops was very small.
It did not swim as fast as the others.
It got left behind.

A big crocodile swung its tail,
and came up beside the baby.

But then a big triceratops
at the side of the herd saw the crocodile.

The triceratops moved quickly.
He put his head down.
He tossed the crocodile
into the air with his big horns,
just in time!

Then the baby swam
to the middle of the herd.

The big triceratops
kept the crocodiles away,
and all the herd
got safely across the river.

The triceratops kept walking along together until at last they came to a green forest. And once again
they had lots of leaves to eat.